BENEATH THE SURFACE

by Shelley Husband

Crochet Blanket Pattern

Copyright © 2019 by Shelley Husband

All rights reserved. No part of this publication may be reproduced or transmitted by any means, electronic, photocopying or otherwise without prior written permission of the author.

ISBN: 978-0-6483497-3-0

Charts made by Amy Gunderson
Email: kinglouiespizza@gmail.com
Ravelry ID: AmyGunderson

Graphic Design by Michelle Lorimer
Email: hello@michellelorimer.com

Photography by Shelley Husband

Technical Editing by SiewBee Pond
Email: essbee1995@yahoo.com

First edition 2019

Published by Shelley Husband

PO Box 11
Narrawong VIC 3285
Australia
www.spincushions.com

Other titles by Shelley Husband

Print & eBook

Granny Square Flair - 50 Fresh, Modern Variations of the Classic Crochet Square
Siren's Atlas - An Ocean of Granny Squares to Crochet

eBooks by Shelley Husband

More than a Granny - 20 Versatile Crochet Patterns
Granny Square Crochet for Beginners - free ebook
Flowers Abound - 20 Floral Crochet Patterns
GREG Crochet Blanket Pattern
FRAN Crochet Blanket Pattern
More than a Granny 2 - 20 Fun, New Crochet Patterns
Kaboom Crochet Blanket Pattern
Mayan Crochet Blanket Pattern

Contents

Hello! 4
    What is the Beneath the Surface Crochet Blanket? 4

You will need 5

Help 7

Patterns 9
    Plain Square 10
    Puff Square 11
    Popcorn Square 12
    Prodigious Square 13

Surface Crochet 15

Joining 16

Border Pattern 18

Charts 19
    Plain Square 19
    Puff Square 20
    Popcorn Square 21
    Prodigious Square 22
    Border 26

Hints and Tips 27
    Plain Square 27
    Puff Square 27
    Popcorn Square 28
    Prodigious Square 29

Round by Round Photos 31
    Plain Square 31
    Puff Square 32
    Popcorn Square 33
    Prodigious Square 34

About the Author 37

Hello!

Thanks so much for choosing to make my Beneath the Surface Crochet Blanket Pattern. I hope you learn lots and have a great time making your blanket.

What is the Beneath the Surface Crochet Blanket?

An exercise in calm, the Beneath the Surface Crochet Blanket is a solid, simple yet effective blanket for your home.

This is a project perfect for the adventurous beginner, with only the simplest of stitches used to make the solid base of the blanket. After the squares are made, surface crochet is added in a contrasting colour to make the circles and squares on top.

The blanket measures 162 cm/64 in square.

Any crocheter with basic skills will enjoy this crochet adventure. If you can make a granny square, you can make the Beneath the Surface Crochet Blanket. I will be at your side every step of the way with step by step instructions and videos available for each round of the pattern on my YouTube channel. You'll also find charts for all parts included.

You will make the several of each of the smaller squares and one large Prodigious square and, after joining them, add a simple border.

You will need

Here are all the things you will need to make your own Beneath the Surface Crochet Blanket.

You'll need a yarn needle and a pair of scissors, of course. Then there's your yarn and hook. What specific yarn and hook you use is up to you.

The information here is what I used. I have also provided some information that may assist if you'd like to use a different yarn.

Yarn

The Beneath the Surface Crochet Blanket is a very yarn hungry, solid blanket, I really do recommend you use a light weight yarn. Cotton is perfect. You see, the blanket is very heavy, even in cotton – almost 2 kilograms. If you use wool or another heavier yarn, your blanket may be just too heavy, and you will need a lot more yarn. It will also be much larger. Of course, it's up to you what yarn you use. I just wanted to make all that clear up front.

Ideally, your yarn should match as closely as possible the Bendigo Woollen Mills 8 ply cotton I used. If you are outside of Australia, www.yarnsub.com is a great website that compares yarns. If you search Bendigo Woollen Mills 8 ply cotton, it will give you some almost perfect matches that you can get pretty much anywhere in the world.

If you want to do your own research and comparison, here are the BWM 8 ply cotton properties:

Weight:	DK / Light Worsted
Texture:	Plied
Fibre:	Cotton (100%)
Hook:	4 mm (6 or G US) (8 UK)
Gauge:	22 sts / 10 cm (4 in)
Balls:	200 g; 485 m (529 yds)
Metres/Gram:	2.43 m/g (2.65 yds/g)

Hook

The hook size recommended for the Bendigo Woollen Mills 8 ply cotton is 4 mm.

Colours

The Beneath the Surface Crochet Blanket is made with one main colour and a contrasting colour for the surface crochet. You can do whatever you want though!

For my blanket, I used Bendigo Woollen Mills 8 ply cotton yarn in Glacier for the base of all squares and used the same yarn in Storm Cloud for the surface crochet.

To try out colour combinations, try the mini taster pattern on page 9.

How much yarn do I need?

To make a blanket like my sample 162 cm (64 in) square blanket using 8 ply Bendigo Woollen Mills cotton, you'll need approximately:

Main colour: 7 or 8 balls, 200 grams each (I used Glacier)

Surface crochet: 3 balls, 200 grams each (I used Storm Cloud)

If you use a different yarn or even just a different hook size, you may need more or less yarn and your blanket will likely be a different size too.

The difference in how much yarn you will need can be quite significant.

For example, this is the same pattern, made by me with the same hook. The larger blue Plain square is made with Bendigo Woollen Mills Classic 8 ply wool. The other is made with Bendigo Woollen Mills 8 ply cotton. There are 2 metres per gram in this wool and 2.43 metres per gram in the cotton.

As you can see, the wool version is quite a bit larger – half an inch bigger. It also used a lot more yarn.

The blue wool version (using weight as the basis for the calculations) used 57 metres in total while the cotton version used 46 metres in total. When you consider that this square is made 32 times, then the extra yarn needed just for this square is 352 metres. That's almost an extra 200 gram ball to make all the Plain squares in the pattern. Then add the extra you'll need for the other squares, joining and border and you can see how a lot more yarn will be required than what I used.

How do I work out how much of my yarn of choice I need?

So what do you do if you're using a different yarn?

Well, you'll have to do some calculations. First up you need something to compare to, so I have listed below how many metres of Bendigo Woollen Mills Cotton I used for each of the squares in the whole blanket. (I have slightly overstated these figures.)

4 ply (fingering)

Plain: 35 metres + 6 metres for surface crochet (38.28 yards + 6.56 yards)

Puff: 42 metres + 6 metres for surface crochet (45.93 yards + 6.56 yards)

Popcorn: 48 metres + 6 metres for surface crochet (52.49 yards + 6.56 yards)

Prodigious: 310 metres + 40 metres for surface crochet (339.02 yards + 43.74 yards)

8 ply (DK/light worsted)

Plain: 41 metres + 7 metres for surface crochet (44.84 yards + 7.66 yards)

Puff: 48 metres + 7 metres for surface crochet (52.49 yards + 7.66 yards)

Popcorn: 57 metres + 7 metres for surface crochet (62.34 yards + 7.65 yards)

Prodigious: 370 metres + 46 metres for surface crochet (404.64 yards + 50.31 yards)

10 ply (aran/worsted)

Plain: 50 metres + 8 metres for surface crochet (54.68 yards + 8.75 yards)

Puff: 57 metres + 8 metres for surface crochet (62.34 yards + 8.75 yards)

Popcorn: 66 metres + 8 metres for surface crochet (72.18 yards + 8.75 yards)

Prodigious: 456 metres + 50 metres for surface crochet (498.69 yards + 54.68 yards)

Next, you need to make one of the Plain squares in your yarn of choice. Weigh it, then using the information on your yarn label, calculate how many metres you used.

If it's much the same or less than my measurements, all is well. Use my yardage calculations for the whole blanket.

If it's more, then you'll need to figure out how much extra yarn you'll need by testing the other squares as well. For the big one, as there's only one to be made, compare the differences between my figures and yours for the other squares and see what approximate percentage more is used. Apply that to my Prodigious yardage to work out roughly how much extra you'll need.

You will need to make 32 Plain squares, 24 Puff squares and 16 Popcorn squares, as well as one Prodigious square. Plus you'll need extra for joining and the border.

Help

If you just want to get stuck in and crochet, you'll find the written pattern without extra info begin on page 10. If you need help, go to the Charts on page 19, Hints and Tips on page 27 or the Round by Round Photos on page 31.

There are also videos for each pattern, the surface crochet and joining on my YouTube Channel. Search for "spincushions" on YouTube and you'll find my channel. Then look for the Beneath the Surface Playlist for all the videos.

Here are a few tips for the pattern in general.

How do I read your patterns?

If this is the first time you are using my patterns, head to my blog www.spincushions.com and search "how to read my patterns". This post has explanations of all the reasons for the asterisks, repeats, brackets and abbreviations.

Magic Circle

Instead of chaining and making a loop to work into, I like to begin with a magic circle as you can pull it really tightly closed. You do have to be very diligent sewing in your ends though, so remember that if you choose to use a magic circle.

False stitch instead of ch3 starting chain

In the patterns, at the beginning of some rounds, I have used the standard "ch3" as a starting chain in place of the first stitch. In reality, I use a false stitch instead. It is a little fiddly to begin with, but I think it looks much better. I have a video on my YouTube channel showing how it's done. You don't have to do it if the starting chain doesn't bother you. It's really ok.

Surface Crochet

This may be something new to you, but it's not tricky. You can do it. I find it quite therapeutic to do. Such a gentle rhythmic action.

Weave in your ends as you go. Trust me on this. Do you really want to have to deal with over 500 ends just from the surface crochet at the end? I sure don't!

When weaving in the ends, check your work from the front to make sure you can't see the needle before you pull the yarn tail through or you'll see your yarn from the front.

If you find your squares are still very wobbly after the surface crochet, try using a smaller hook to do the surface crochet. If you find your squares are pulled in too tight, try using a larger hook to do the surface crochet.

You will see the surface crochet yarn on the back. Here's what one of my Plain squares looks like from the back.

General Tips

Check your stitch counts regularly to make sure you're on track. It can all look fine but once you start to square off, it just won't work if you have the wrong number of stitches.

Blocking

Blocking is a little trick that helps make your work look a lot better. I do it very simply by pinning each block to a foam board and squirting it with steam from my iron. Job done! I made a blocking board myself by ruling lines on a foam mat. There are heaps of varieties of them available online if you'd rather have a ready-to-go blocking board.

I blocked my small squares to 16.5 cm (6.5 in) and the Prodigious square to 51 cm (20 in).

Ok, let's start.

Patterns

Mini Taster Pattern

This small square pattern is to help you choose your colours and have a play with a few different options.

Abbreviations

R	Round
ss	slip stitch
sp/s	space/s
st/s	stitch/es
ch	chain
cnr/s	corner/s
stch	starting chain
dc	double crochet
htr	half treble crochet
tr	treble crochet
hdtr	half double treble crochet
dtr	double treble crochet

The Mini Taster Pattern

Begin with a magic circle or ch4 and join the last ch to the first with a ss to make a loop.

R1: ch3 (stch), 15tr, join with ss to 3rd ch of stch. {16 sts}

R2: ch3 (stch), tr in same st as ss, 2tr in next 15 sts, join with ss to 3rd ch of stch. {32 sts}

R3: ch4 (stch), hdtr in same st as ss, *tr in next st, htr in next st, dc in next 3 sts, htr in next st, tr in next st**, (2hdtr, dtr, 2hdtr) in next st*, repeat from * to * 2x & * to ** 1x, 2hdtr in same st as first sts, join with ss to 4th ch of stch. {11 sts on each side; 4 1-st cnrs}

R4: dc in same st as ss, *dc in next 11 sts**, (dc, ch2, dc) in next st*, repeat from * to * 2x & * to ** 1x, dc in same st as first st, ch2, join with ss to first st. Fasten off. {13 sts on each side; 4 2-ch cnr sps}

Surface Crochet.

Working from the front of the square, pull your contrasting colour yarn to the front from behind between any sts of R1. Work a ss around all but the last st of R1. Fasten off with invisible join to first ss. On back, tie ends together and then weave ends in.

Repeat for R2 & R3.

Plain Square

You will need to make 32 of these squares.

Abbreviations

R	Round
ss	slip stitch
sp/s	space/s
st/s	stitch/es
cnr/s	corner/s
ch	chain
stch	starting chain
dc	double crochet
htr	half treble crochet
tr	treble crochet
hdtr	half double treble crochet
dtr	double treble crochet

Plain Square Pattern

Begin with a magic circle or ch4 and join the last ch to the first with a ss to make a loop.

R1: ch3 (stch), 15tr, join with ss to 3rd ch of stch. {16 sts}

R2: ch3 (stch), tr in same st as ss, *tr in next st**, 2tr in next st*, repeat from * to * 6x & * to ** 1x, join with ss to 3rd ch of stch. {24 sts}

R3: ch3 (stch), tr in next st, *2tr in next 4 sts**, tr in next 2 sts*, repeat from * to * 2x & * to ** 1x, join with ss to 3rd ch of stch. {40 sts}

R4: ch3 (stch), *2tr in next st**, tr in next st*, repeat from * to * 18x & * to ** 1x, join with ss to 3rd ch of stch. {60 sts}

R5: ch3 (stch), tr in next 3 sts, *2tr in next 2 sts**, tr in next 4 sts*, repeat from * to * 8x & * to ** 1x, join with ss to 3rd ch of stch. {80 sts}

R6: ch4 (stch), 2hdtr in same st as ss, *tr in next 3 sts, htr in next 4 sts, dc in next 5 sts, htr in next 4 sts, tr in next 3 sts**, (2hdtr, dtr, 2hdtr) in next st*, repeat from * to * 2x & * to ** 1x, 2hdtr in same st as first sts, join with ss to 4th ch of stch. {23 sts on each side; 4 1-st cnrs}

R7: ch3 (stch), tr in same st as ss, *tr in next 23 sts**, (tr, hdtr, tr) in next st*, repeat from * to * 2x & * to ** 1x, tr in same st as first sts, join with ss to 3rd ch of stch. {25 sts on each side; 4 1-st cnrs}

R8: dc in same st as ss, *dc in next 25 sts**, (dc, ch2, dc) in next st*, repeat from * to * 2x & * to ** 1x, dc in same st as first st, ch2, join with ss to first st. Fasten off. {27 sts on each side; 4 2-ch cnr sps}

Note: It will be a bit wobbly at this point. Adding the surface crochet flattens it out. Blocking after the surface crochet is recommended.

Surface Crochet

Working from the front of the square, pull your contrasting colour yarn to the front from behind between any sts of R1. Work a ss around all but the last st of R1. Fasten off with invisible join to first ss. On back, tie ends together and then weave ends in.

Repeat for R3, R5 & R7.

Puff Square

You will need to make 24 of these squares.

Abbreviations

R	Round
ss	slip stitch
sp/s	space/s
st/s	stitch/es
cnr/s	corner/s
ch	chain
stch	starting chain
dc	double crochet
htr	half treble crochet
tr	treble crochet
hdtr	half double treble crochet
dtr	double treble crochet
puff	puff stitch = 4htr puff – 4x [yo, insert hook in st, pull up a loop], yo, pull through all loops on hook
fp	front post

Puff Square Pattern

Begin with a magic circle or ch4 and join the last ch to the first with a ss to make a loop.

R1: ch3 (stch), 15tr, join with ss to 3rd ch of stch. {16 sts}

R2: ch3 (stch), *puff in next st**, 2tr in next st*, repeat from * to * 6x & * to ** 1x, tr in same st as first st, join with ss to 3rd ch of stch. {24 sts}

R3: ch3 (stch), tr in same st as ss, *fptr around next st**, 2tr in next 2 sts*, repeat from * to * 6x & * to ** 1x, 2tr in next st, join with ss to 3rd ch of stch. {40 sts}

R4: dc in same st as ss, dc in next 39 sts, join with ss to first st. {40 sts}

R5: ch3 (stch), tr in same st as ss, *puff in next st**, 3tr in next st*, repeat from * to * 18x & * to ** 1x, tr in same st as first sts, join with ss to 3rd ch of stch. {80 sts}

R6: ch3 (stch), tr in next st, *fptr around next st**, tr in next 3 sts*, repeat from * to * 18x & * to ** 1x, tr in next st, join with ss to 3rd ch of stch. {80 sts}

R7: ch2 (not counted in stitch count), puff in same st as ss, *ch1, puff in next st, ch1, tr in next 3 sts, htr in next 3 sts, dc in next 5 sts, htr in next 3 sts, tr in next 3 sts, ch1, puff in next st, ch1**, puff in next st*, repeat from * to * 2x & * to ** 1x, join with ss to first puff. {19 sts, 4 1-ch sps on each side; 4 1-st cnrs}

R8: fpss around puff below, ch4 (stch), *2dtr in 1-ch sp, fphdtr around next st, tr in 1-ch sp, htr in next 3 sts, dc in next 11 sts, htr in next 3 sts, tr in 1-ch sp, fphdtr around next st, 2dtr in 1-ch sp**, fpdtr around next st*, repeat from * to * 2x & * to ** 1x, join with ss to 4th ch of stch. {25 sts on each side; 4 1-st cnrs}

R9: dc in same st as ss, *dc in next 25 sts**, (dc, ch2, dc) in next st*, repeat from * to * 2x & * to ** 1x, dc in same st as first st, ch2, join with ss to first st. Fasten off. {27 sts on each side; 4 2-ch cnr sps}

Note: It will be a bit wobbly at this point. Adding the surface crochet flattens it out. Blocking after the surface crochet is recommended.

Surface Crochet

Working from the front of the square, pull your contrasting colour yarn to the front from behind between any sts of R1. Work a ss around all but the last st of R1. Fasten off with invisible join to first ss. On back, tie ends together and then weave ends in.

Repeat for R3, R6 & R8.

Popcorn Square

You will need to make 16 of these squares.

Abbreviations

R	Round
ss	slip stitch
sp/s	space/s
st/s	stitch/es
cnr/s	corner/s
ch	chain
stch	starting chain
dc	double crochet
htr	half treble crochet
tr	treble crochet
hdtr	half double treble crochet
dtr	double treble crochet

Popcorn Square Pattern

Begin with a magic circle or ch4 and join the last ch to the first with a ss to make a loop.

R1: ch3 (stch), 15tr, join with ss to 3rd ch of stch. {16 sts}

R2: ch3 (stch), *ch1, 5tr in next st, ch1**, tr in next st*, repeat from * to * 6x & * to ** 1x, join with ss to 3rd ch of stch. {48 sts, 16 1-ch sps}

R3: dc in same st as ss, *dc in 1-ch sp, dc in both the 1-ch sps on either side of the next 5 sts at same time, dc in 1-ch sp**, dc in next st*, repeat from * to * 6x & * to ** 1x, join with ss to first st. {32 sts}

R4: ch3 (stch), tr in next st, *2tr in next st**, tr in next 3 sts*, repeat from * to * 6x & * to ** 1x, tr in next st, join with ss to 3rd ch of stch. {40 sts}

R5: ch3 (stch), *ch1, 5tr in next st, ch1**, tr in next st*, repeat from * to * 18x & * to ** 1x, join with ss to 3rd ch of stch. {120 sts, 40 1-ch sps}

R6: dc in same st as ss, *dc in 1-ch sp, dc in both the 1-ch sps on either side of the next 5 sts at same time, dc in 1-ch sp**, dc in next st*, repeat from * to * 18x & * to ** 1x, join with ss to first st. {80 sts}

R7: ch3 (stch), 4tr in same st as ss, *ch1, 5tr in next st, ch1, tr in next 3 sts, htr in next 3 sts, dc in next 5 sts, htr in next 3 sts, tr in next 3 sts, ch1, 5tr in next st, ch1**, 5tr in next st*, repeat from * to * 2x & * to ** 1x, join with ss to 3rd ch of stch. {27 sts, 4 1-ch sps on each side; 4 5-st cnrs}

R8: dc in both the 1-ch sps on either side of the next 5 sts at the same time, *dc in 1-ch sp, dc in both the 1-ch sps on either side of the next 5 sts at same time, dc in 1-ch sp, dc in next 17 sts, dc in 1-ch sp, dc in both the 1-ch sps on either side of the next 5 sts at same time, dc in 1-ch sp**, dc in both the 1-ch sps on either side of next 5 sts at the same time*, repeat from * to * 2x & * to ** 1x, join with ss to first st. {23 sts on each side; 4 1-st cnrs}

R9: ch4 (stch), dtr in same st as ss, *hdtr in next 2 sts, tr in next 19 sts, hdtr in next 2 sts**, 3dtr in next st*, repeat from * to * 2x & * to ** 1x, dtr in same st as first sts, join with ss to 4th ch of stch. {23 sts on each side; 4 3-st cnrs}

R10: dc in same st as ss, *dc in next 25 sts**, (dc, ch2, dc) in next st*, repeat from * to * 2x & * to ** 1x, dc in same sp as first st, ch2, join with ss to first st. Fasten off. {27 sts on each side; 4 2-ch cnr sps}

Note: It will be a bit wobbly at this point. Adding the surface crochet flattens it out. Blocking after the surface crochet is recommended.

Surface Crochet

Working from the front of the square, pull your contrasting colour yarn to the front from behind between any sts of R1. Work a ss around all but the last st of R1. Fasten off with invisible join to first ss. On back, tie ends together and then weave ends in.

Repeat for R4, R6 & R9.

Prodigious Square

You will need to make 1 square.

Abbreviations

R	Round
ss	slip stitch
sp/s	space/s
st/s	stitch/es
cnr/s	corner/s
ch	chain
stch	starting chain
dc	double crochet
htr	half treble crochet
tr	treble crochet
hdtr	half double treble crochet
dtr	double treble crochet
puff	puff stitch = 4htr puff – 4x [yo, insert hook in st, pull up a loop], yo, pull through all loops on hook
fp	front post

Prodigious Square Pattern

Begin with a magic circle or ch4 and join the last ch to the first with a ss to make a loop.

R1: ch3 (stch), 15tr, join with ss to 3rd ch of stch. {16 sts}

R2: ch3 (stch), tr in same st as ss, *tr in next st**, 2tr in next st*, repeat from * to * 6x & * to ** 1x, join with ss to 3rd ch of stch. {24 sts}

R3: ch3 (stch), tr in next st, *2tr in next 4 sts**, tr in next 2 sts*, repeat from * to * 2x & * to ** 1x, join with ss to 3rd ch of stch. {40 sts}

R4: ch3 (stch), *2tr in next st**, tr in next st*, repeat from * to * 18x & * to ** 1x, join with ss to 3rd ch of stch. {60 sts}

R5: ch3 (stch), tr in next 3 sts, *2tr in next 2 sts**, tr in next 4 sts, repeat from * to * 8x * to ** 1x, join with ss to 3rd ch of stch. {80 sts}

R6: dc in same st as ss, dc in next 79 sts, join with ss to first st. {80 sts}

R7: ch3 (stch), tr in next 79 sts, join with ss to 3rd ch of stch. {80 sts}

R8: dc in same st as ss, dc in next 79 sts, join with ss to first st. {80 sts}

R9: ch3 (stch), tr in same st as ss, 2tr in next st, *tr in next 6 sts**, 2tr in next 2 sts*, repeat from * to * 8x & * to ** 1x, join with ss to 3rd ch of stch. {100 sts}

R10: ch3 (stch), tr in same st as ss, *puff in next st**, 2tr in next st*, repeat from * to * 48x & * to ** 1x, join with ss to 3rd ch of stch. {150 sts}

R11: ch3 (stch), tr in next st, *fptr around next st**, tr in next 2 sts*, repeat from * to * 48x & * to ** 1x, join with ss to 3rd ch of stch. {150 sts}

R12: dc in same st as ss, dc in next 149 sts, join with ss to first st. {150 sts}

R13: ch3 (stch), tr in next 149 sts, join with ss to 3rd ch of stch. {150 sts}

R14: dc in same st as ss, dc in next 149 sts, join with ss to first st. {150 sts}

R15: ch3 (stch), tr in same st as ss, *tr in next 4 sts**, 2tr in next st*, repeat from * to * 28x & * to ** 1x, join with ss to 3rd ch of stch. {180 sts}

R16: ch3 (stch), tr in next st, 2tr in next st, tr in next 2 sts, *ch1, 5tr in next st, ch1**, tr in next 2 sts, 2tr in next st, tr in next 2 sts*, repeat from * to * 28x & * to ** 1x, join with ss to 3rd ch of stch. {330 sts, 60 1-ch sps}

R17: dc in same st as ss, dc in next 5 sts, *dc in both the 1-ch sps on either side of the next 5 sts at same time**, dc in next 6 sts*, repeat from * to * 28x & * to ** 1x, join with ss to first st. {210 sts}

R18: ch3 (stch), tr in next 209 sts, join with ss to 3rd ch of stch. {210 sts}

R19: dc in same st as ss, dc in next 209 sts, join with ss to first st. {210 sts}

R20: ch3 (stch), tr in next 209 sts, join with ss to 3rd ch of stch. {210 sts}

R21: dc in same st as ss, dc in next 103 sts, 2dc in next st, dc in next 104 sts, 2dc in next st, join with ss to first st. {212 sts}

R22: ch4 (stch), hdtr in same st as ss, *hdtr in next st, 2hdtr in next st, hdtr in next st, tr in next st, 2tr in next st, tr in next st, 10x [htr in next 3 sts, 2htr in next st], tr in next st, 2tr in next st, tr in next st, hdtr in next st, 2hdtr in next st, hdtr in next st**, (hdtr, dtr, hdtr) in next st*, repeat from * to * 2x & * to ** 1x, hdtr in same st as first sts, join with ss to 4th ch of stch.
{66 sts on each side; 4 3-st cnrs}

R23: ch3 (stch), 4tr in same st as ss, *ch1, 5tr in next st, ch1, 2x [2tr in next st, tr in next st], 3x [ch1, puff in next st], ch1, tr in next 5 sts, htr in next 5 sts, dc in next 32 sts, htr in next 5 sts, tr in next 5 sts, 3x [ch1, puff in next st], ch1, 2x [tr in next st, 2tr in next st], ch1, 5tr in next st, ch1**, 5tr in next st*, repeat from * to * 2x & * to ** 1x, join with ss to 3rd ch of stch.
{80 sts, 12 1-ch sps on each side; 4 5-st cnrs}

R24: ss in both the 1-ch sps on either side of the ch3 (stch) & next 4 sts at same time, ch4 (stch), *dtr in 1-ch sp, dtr in both the 1-ch sps on either side of the next 5 sts at same time, ch1, dtr in 1-ch sp, hdtr in next 6 sts, 3x [skip 1-ch sp, fptr around next st], skip 1-ch sp, htr in next 5 sts, dc in next 42 sts, htr in next 5 sts, 3x [skip 1-ch sp, fptr around next st], skip 1-ch sp, hdtr in next 6 sts, dtr in 1-ch sp, ch1, dtr in both the 1-ch sps on either side of the next 5 sts at same time, dtr in 1-ch sp**, dtr in both the 1-ch sps on either side of the next 5 sts at same time*, repeat from * to * 2x & * to ** 1x, join with ss to 4th ch of stch.
{76 sts, 2 1-ch sps on each side; 4 1-st cnrs}

R25: dc in both the 1-ch sps on either side of the 5dtr sts at same time, *dc in 1-ch sp, dc in next 72 sts, dc in 1-ch sp**, dc in both the 1-ch sps on either side of the next 5 sts at same time*, repeat from * to * 2x & * to ** 1x, join with ss to first st.
{74 sts on each side; 4 1-st cnrs}

R26: ch4 (stch), (hdtr, tr) in same st as ss, *tr in next 74 sts**, (tr, hdtr, dtr, hdtr, tr) in next st*, repeat from * to * 2x & * to ** 1x, (tr, hdtr) in same st as first sts, join with ss to 4th ch of stch. {74 sts on each side; 4 5-st cnrs}

R27: 2dc in same st as ss, *dc in next 78 sts**, 3dc in next st*, repeat from * to * 2x & * to ** 1x, dc in same st as first sts, join with ss to first st.
{78 sts on each side; 4 3-st cnrs}

R28: ch4 (stch), hdtr in same st as ss, *tr in next 80 sts**, (hdtr, dtr, hdtr) in next st*, repeat from * to * 2x & * to ** 1x, hdtr in same st as first sts, join with ss to 4th ch of stch. {80 sts on each side; 4 3-st cnrs}

R29: dc in same st as ss, *dc in next 82 sts**, (dc, ch2, dc) in next st*, repeat from * to * 2x & * to ** 1x, dc in same st as first st, ch2, join with ss to first st. Fasten off.
{84 sts on each side; 4 2-ch cnr sps}

Note: It will be a bit wobbly at this point. Adding the surface crochet flattens it out. Blocking after the surface crochet is recommended.

Surface Crochet

Working from the front of the square, pull your contrasting colour yarn to the front from behind between any sts of R1. Work a ss around all but the last st of R1. Fasten off with invisible join to first ss. On back, tie ends together and then weave ends in.

Repeat for R3, R5, R9, R11, R15, R18, R22, R26 & R28.

Surface Crochet

How to work the Surface Crochet

Working from the front of the square, pull your contrasting colour yarn to the front from behind, between any stitches of the Round.

Work a slip stitch around all but the last stitch of the Round.

Fasten off with invisible join to first slip stitch.

On back, tie ends together and then weave ends in.

Joining

Once the squares are made, it's time to join them all into our blanket. I like to join them in strips, then join those strips together. Here's the order I joined the squares (you can do it however you want).

Looking at the layout graphic below, join the squares in the top and bottom three rows into 1 by 9 square strips. Then join the top three and bottom three strips to form two 27-square (3 by 9 squares) rectangles.

Joining order

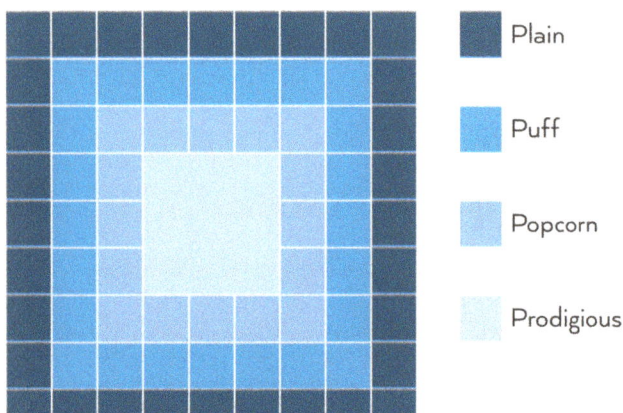

- Plain
- Puff
- Popcorn
- Prodigious

1

2

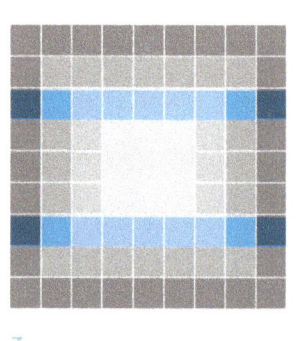

3

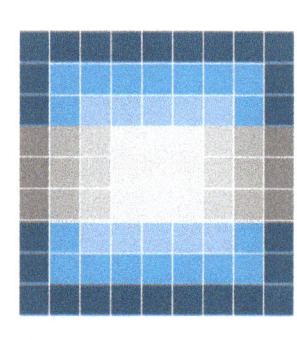

4

For the middle section, join three of each type of square into strips of three, then into two 9-square blocks, then join them to the Prodigious square, making sure the Popcorn squares are next to the Prodigious square (see photo below).

5

6

7

8

Joining method

We are going to join our squares by crocheting them together.

Hold squares right sides together, attach main colour yarn with a standing double crochet to both 2-chain corner spaces on each square at the same time. Work a double crochet into both loops of both squares all the way along, end with a double crochet in both 2-chain corner spaces. Fasten off.

Make sure the Popcorn squares are next to the Prodigious square before you start joining.

Once that's done, you can join your 3 large rectangles into our blanket! Make sure the Plain squares are on the top and bottom of your blanket.

You should end up with your Prodigious square surrounded by Popcorn squares, which are in turn surrounded by Puff squares and the outer edge made of the Plain squares. Magic.

Once you have your strips, here's how to join them.

The joining video on my YouTube channel shows how to join strips together, but here are the written instructions for you:

Join the strips as the squares were joined but when you reach the 2-chain corner spaces, work one stitch in each, ignoring the join. This creates a neat square on the front of the work in the 2-chain corner spaces.

When you are joining the large 9-square blocks to the Prodigious square, there is a 5 stitch difference in stitch counts. There are 5 less stitches on the Prodigious square than the large blocks of 9 squares.

Here's how to deal with that. When you are joining, make sure you do a stitch in each 2-chain space and join. You will also need to use the same stitch twice 5 times on the Prodigious square while using each stitch, chain space and join once on the 9-square blocks. I do a double stitch close to the beginning and end, and space out the other 3 double stitches roughly evenly as I go.

Border Pattern

Once you've joined all your squares, it's time to create the border.

Abbreviations

R	Round
ss	slip stitch
sp/s	space/s
st/s	stitch/es
cnr/s	corner/s
ch	chain
stch	starting chain
stdg dc	standing double crochet
dc	double crochet
tr	treble crochet
hdtr	half double treble crochet

Border Pattern

R1: Attach main colour yarn with a stdg dc to any 2-ch cnr sp, dc in same sp, *dc in each st on side, working a dc in each 2-ch sp and join**, 3dc in 2-ch cnr sp*, rep from * to * 2x and * to ** 1x, dc in same sp as first sts, join with ss to first st.

R2: ch3 (stch), 2tr in same st as ss, *tr in each st on side**, (2tr, hdtr, 2tr) in middle st of 3-st cnr*, rep from * to * 2x and * to ** 1x, 2tr in same st as first sts, join with ss to 3rd ch of stch.

R3: dc in same st as ss, *dc in each st on side**, (dc, ch2, dc) in middle st of 5-st cnr*, rep from * to * 2x and * to ** 1x, dc in same st as first st, ch2, join with ss to first st. Fasten off.

Surface crochet

Working from the front of the square, pull your contrasting colour yarn to the front from behind between any sts of R2. Work a ss around all but the last st of R2. Fasten off with invisible join to first ss. On back, tie ends together and then weave each end around the same colour sts on the back.

Blocking

After you've done your surface crochet, it's a good idea to block your blanket. Yes, it's big and will take a lot of pins, but it really is worth it.

I pinned out my blanket on those big foam mats intended for flooring, all joined up.

It's best to start at one corner and work your way out. Here's mine about half pinned.

When you get to the parts where the squares are joined, add an extra pin to anchor the edge a little way in from the border as well as on the edge. This will help as you stretch the blanket as you pin it all out.

You may need to adjust earlier pins as you go. Once it is all pinned out, squirt it with water and steam from your iron, paying particular attention to the edges. Leave it to dry and voila! One super-duper finished blanket. Well done you!

Charts

On the next few pages, you'll find the Beneath the Surface Crochet Blanket charts.

Plain Square

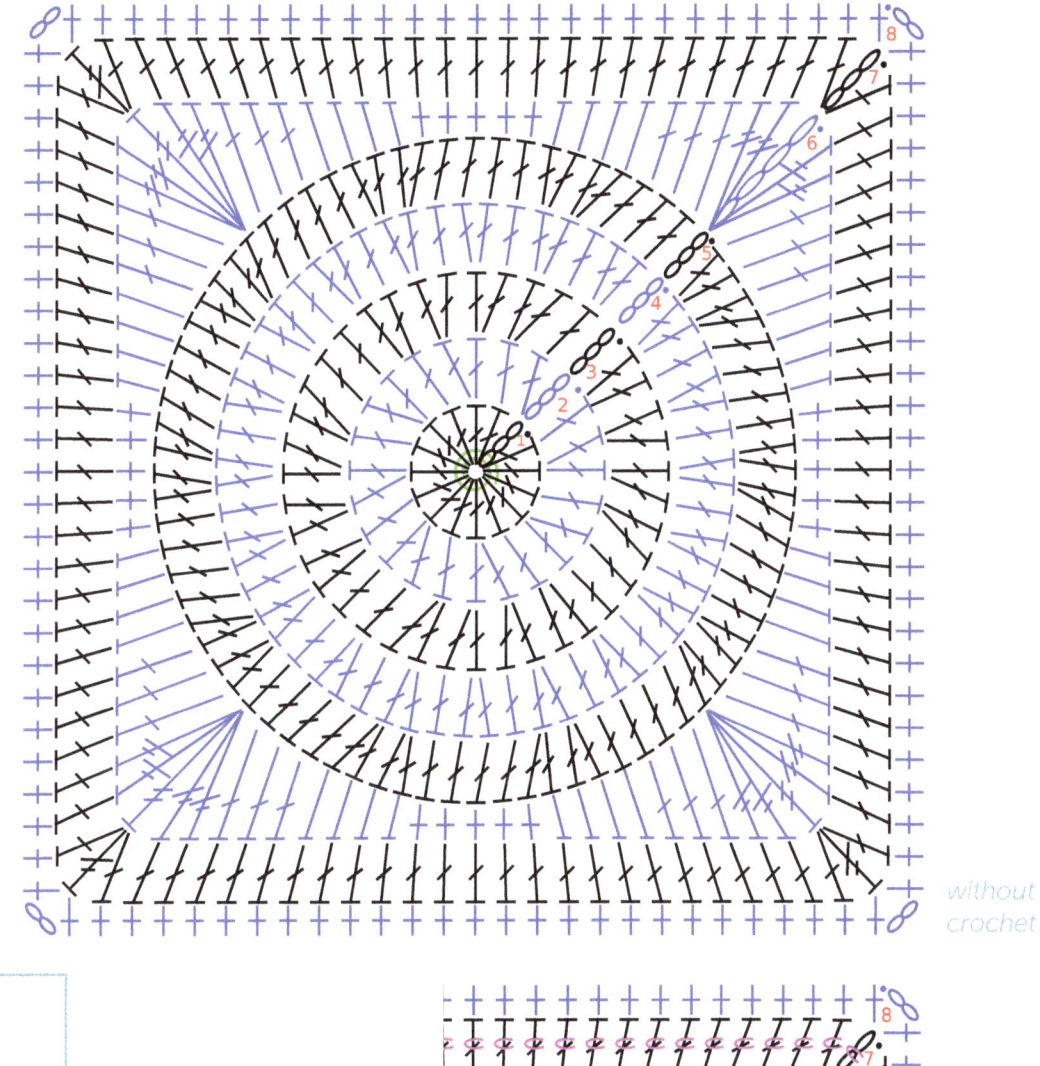

without surface crochet

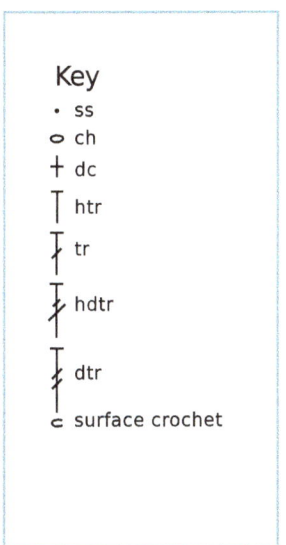

Key
- ss
- ch
- dc
- htr
- tr
- hdtr
- dtr
- surface crochet

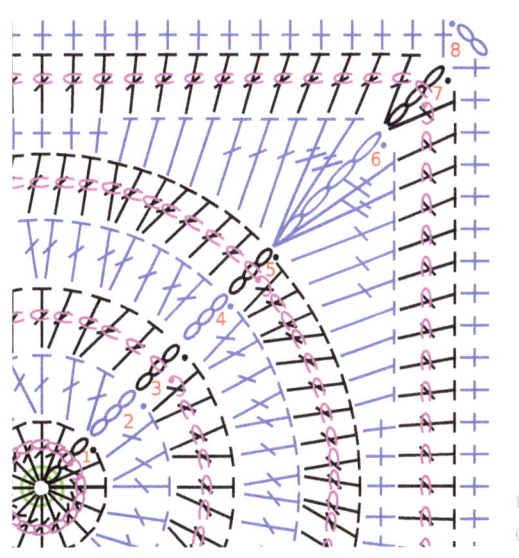

with surface crochet

Puff Square

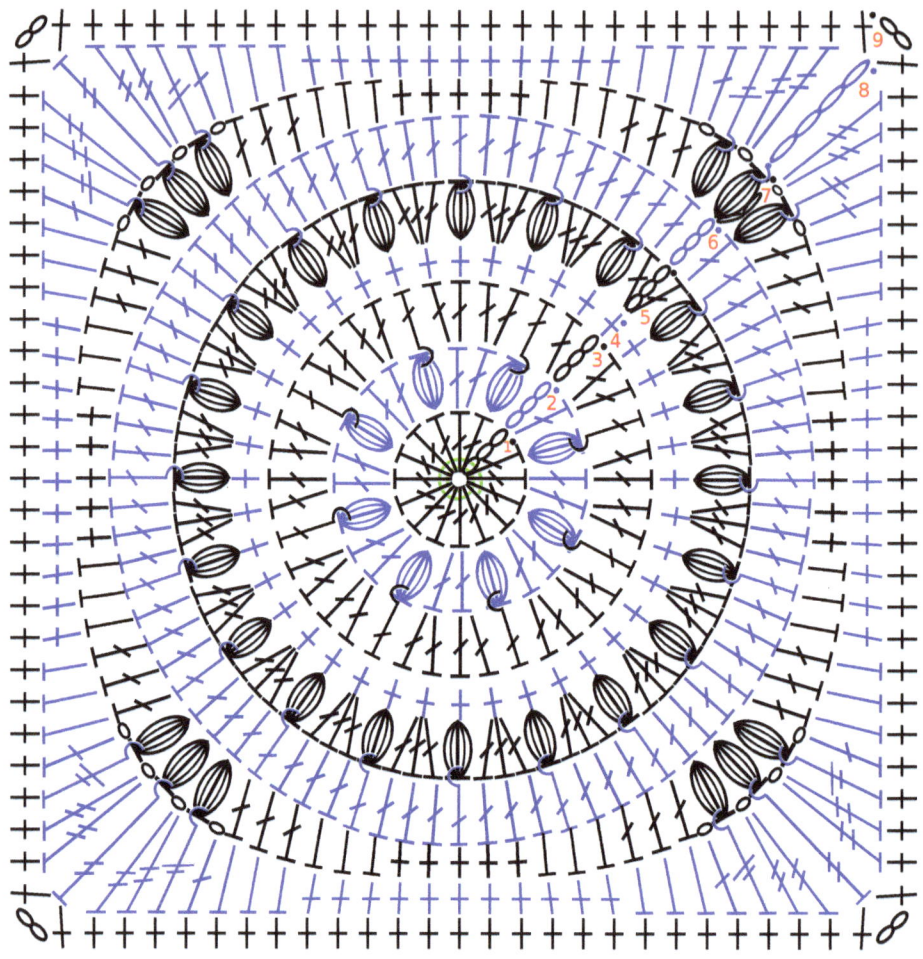

without surface crochet

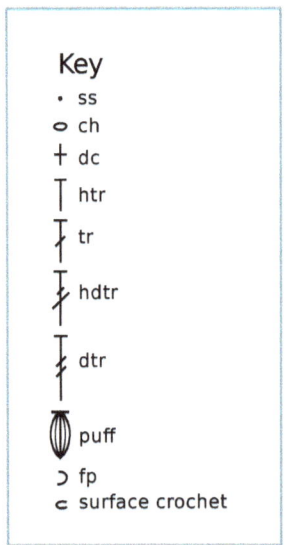

Key
- ss
- ch
- dc
- htr
- tr
- hdtr
- dtr
- puff
- fp
- surface crochet

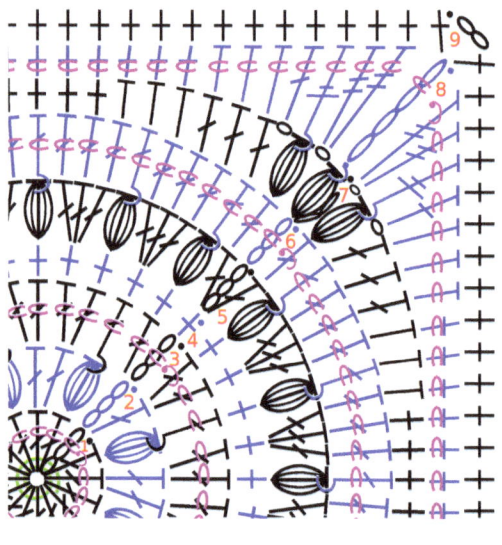

with surface crochet

Popcorn Square

without surface crochet

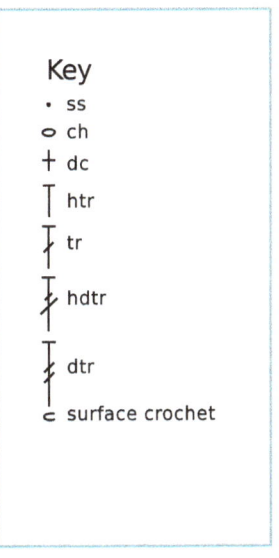

Key
- ss
- ch
- dc
- htr
- tr
- hdtr
- dtr
- surface crochet

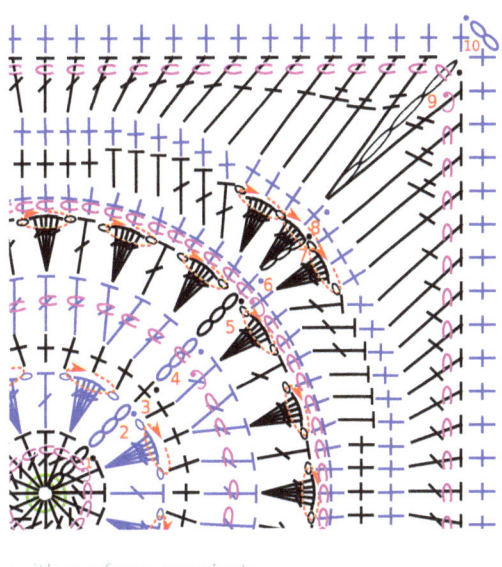

with surface crochet

Prodigious Square
without surface crochet
Rounds 1-10

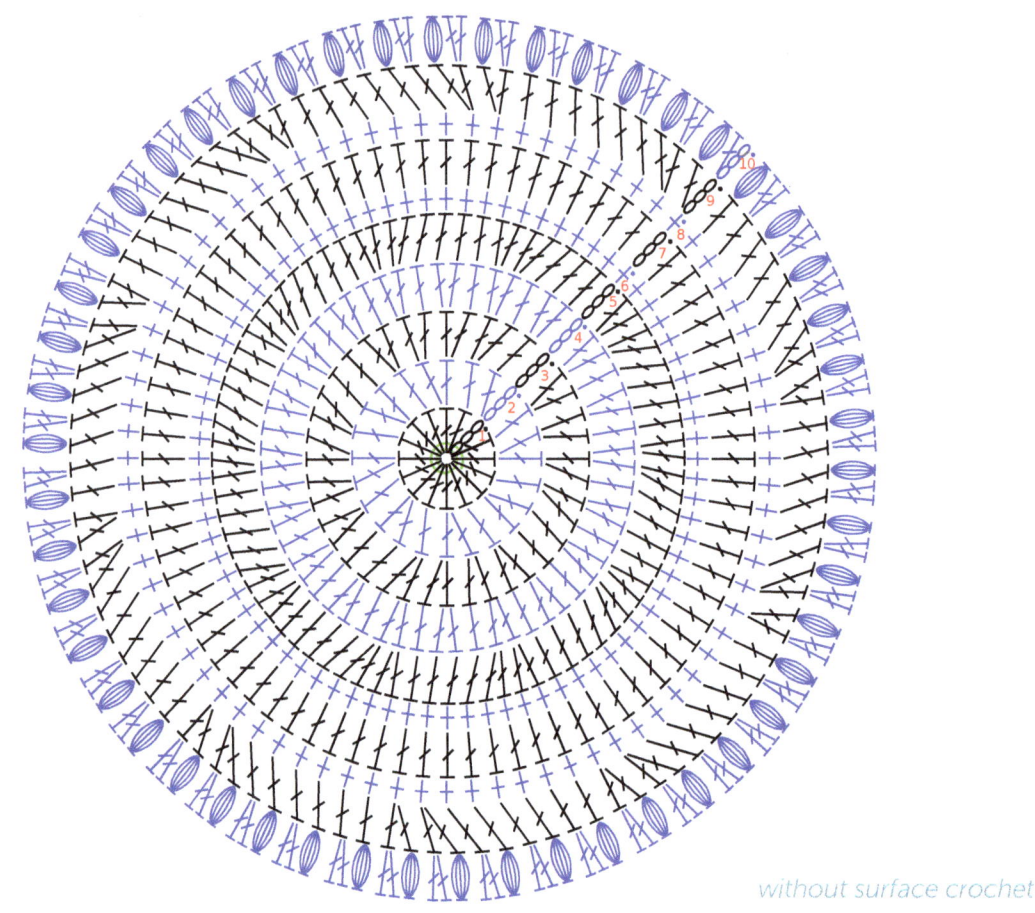

without surface crochet

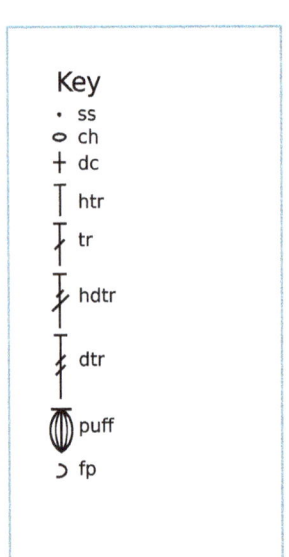

Key
- • ss
- ○ ch
- + dc
- T htr
- ⊤ tr
- ⊤ hdtr
- ⊤ dtr
- 🟰 puff
- ⊃ fp

Prodigious Square
without surface crochet
Rounds 10-21

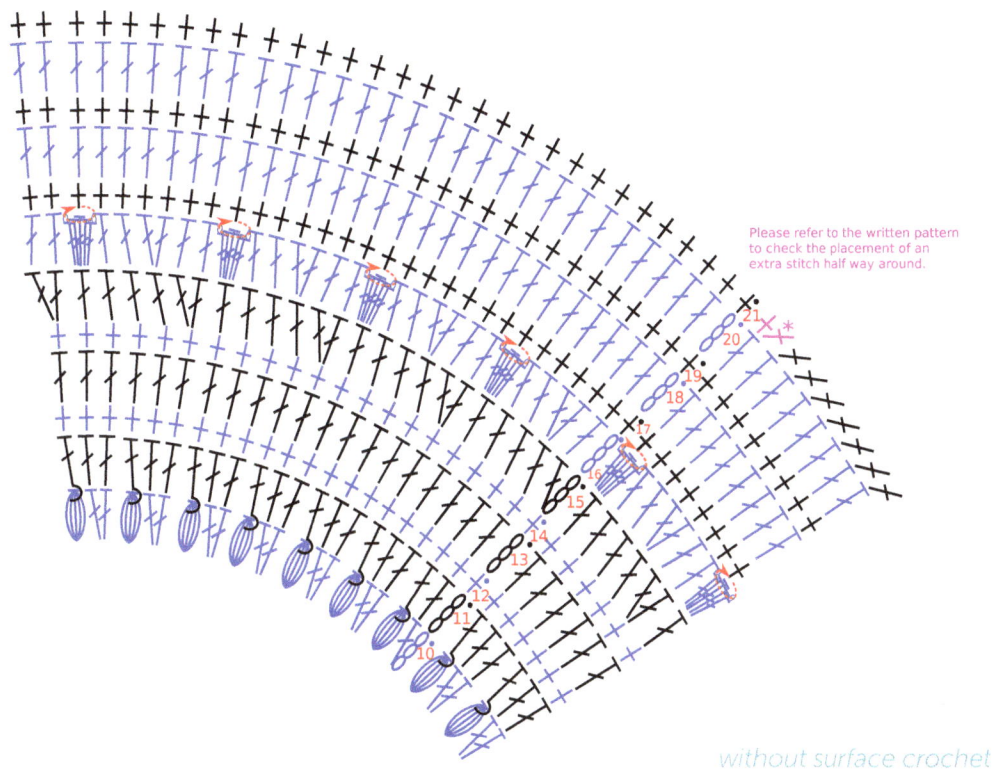

without surface crochet

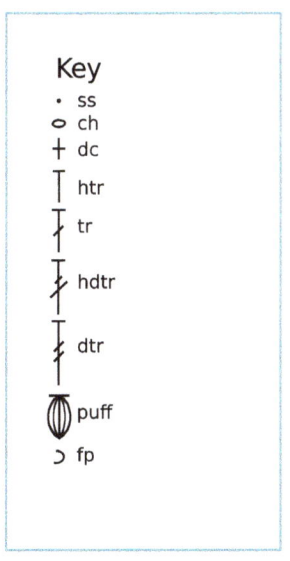

Key
- ss
- ch
- dc
- htr
- tr
- hdtr
- dtr
- puff
- fp

Prodigious Square
without surface crochet
Rounds 21-29

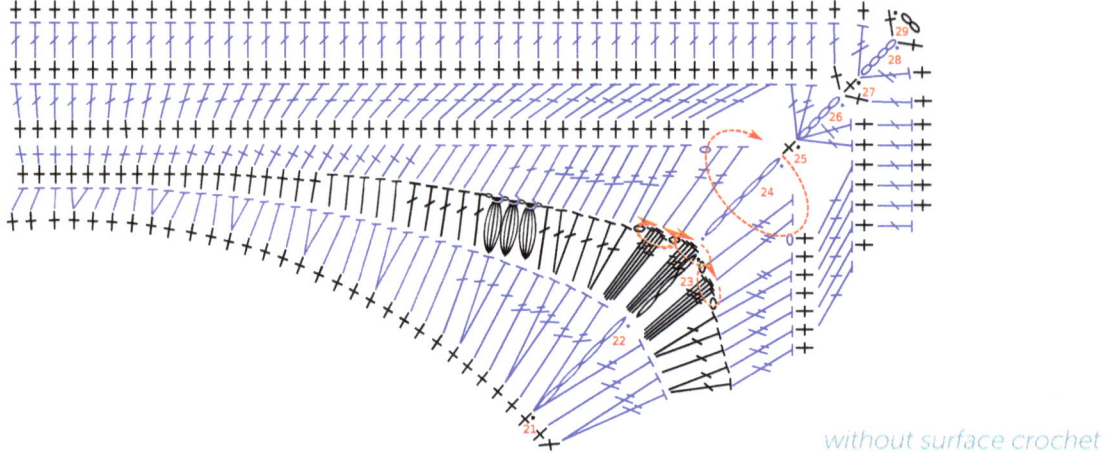

without surface crochet

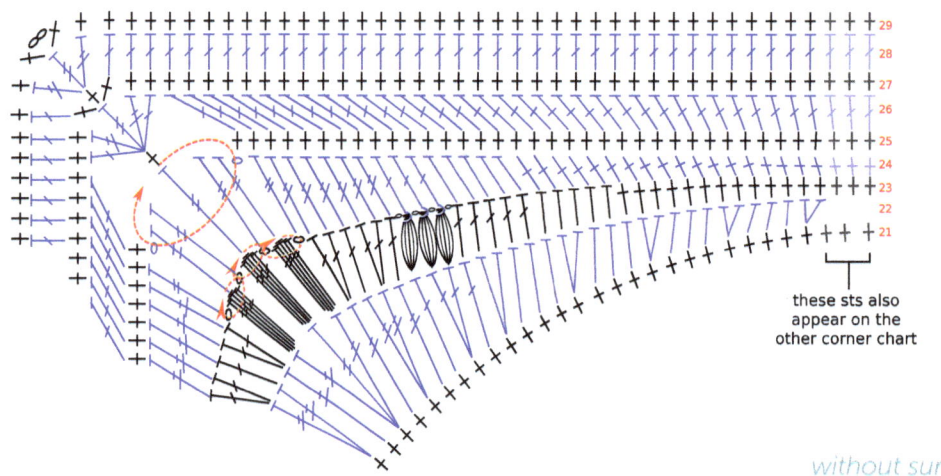

these sts also appear on the other corner chart

without surface crochet

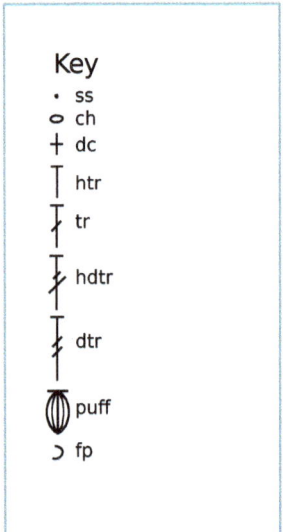

Key
- ss
- ch
- dc
- htr
- tr
- hdtr
- dtr
- puff
- fp

Prodigious Square
surface crochet

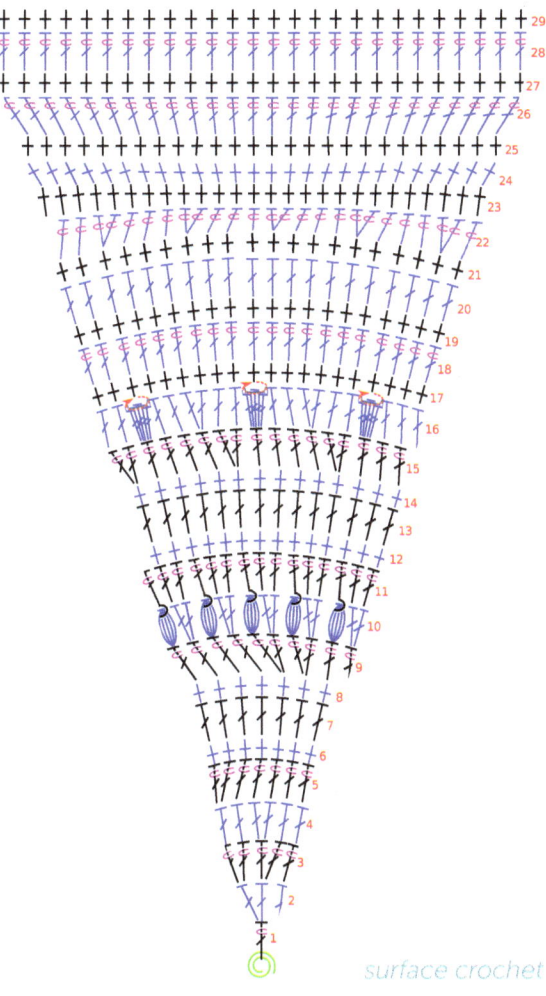

surface crochet

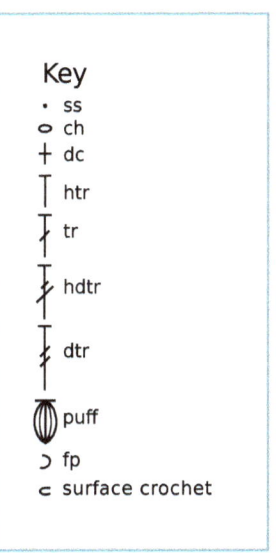

Key
- ss
- ch
- dc
- htr
- tr
- hdtr
- dtr
- puff
- fp
- surface crochet

Border

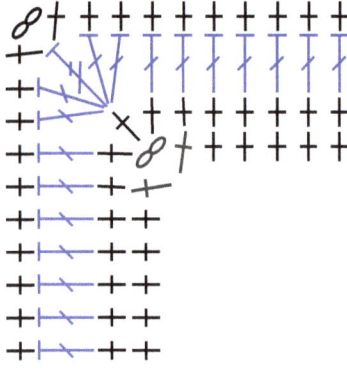
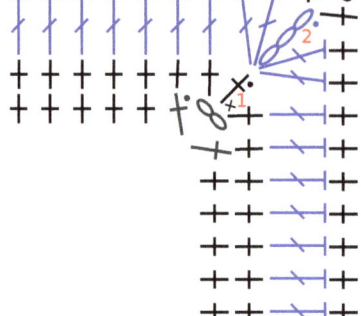

without surface crochet

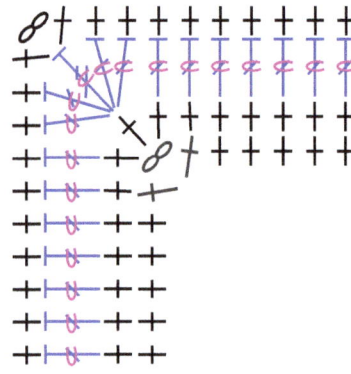
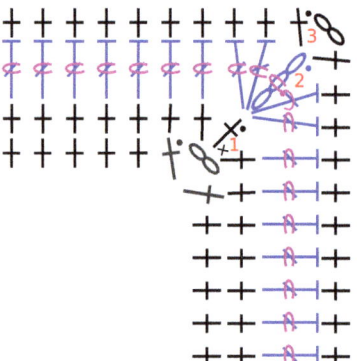

with surface crochet

Key
- ss
- o ch
- + dc
- tr
- hdtr
- c surface crochet

Hints and Tips

Here's where you'll find hints and tips with explanations for any parts that may have you scratching your head if you've never done them before. Check my YouTube video for each pattern if you need more clarification of anything.

Plain Square

Super wobbly, not flat squares

Don't worry! Once you do the surface crochet, your squares will pull in to almost flat. A quick blocking will make them really straight and square.

This is perfectly normal! See my progress shot here? Wobbly, then not so wobbly after the surface crochet, then lovely and square after blocking.

Blocking

When blocking, these squares tend to need a pin in each corner first, then a couple more on each side close to the corner to square them nicely.

Puff Square

Puff Stitches

Puff stitches can be a little tricky, but if you follow my tips, I'm sure you can do them:

- pull up long loops as you make the stitch;
- when pulling through all those loops, pull up with your hook and at the same time, pull down on your work with your other hand and slowly wriggle the hook through all the loops.

Super wobbly, not flat squares

Don't worry! Once you do the surface crochet, your squares will pull in to almost flat. A quick blocking will make them really straight and square.

This is perfectly normal! See my progress shot here? Wobbly, then not so wobbly after the surface crochet, then lovely and square after blocking.

Blocking

These squares tend to need a pin in each corner first, then a couple more on each side close to the corner to square them nicely.

Popcorn Square

Popcorn Stitches

I make my popcorn stitches a little differently to how you may be used to doing them. I do them the lazy way. What that means is there is no taking your hook out to make a popcorn. The popcorns are made over 2 rounds. The first step is to make groups of 5 stitches with a 1-chain space on either side. Then we use those 1-chain spaces to gather the groups of 5 stitches into popcorns in the next round.

The needle in the photo below shows where to put your hook to gather the stitches into a popcorn.

Here's what it looks like after the popcorn is made. Cool huh?

Super wobbly, not flat squares

Don't worry! Once you do the surface crochet, your squares will pull in to almost flat. A quick blocking will make them really straight and square.

This is perfectly normal! See my progress shot here? Wobbly, then not so wobbly after the surface crochet, then lovely and square after blocking.

Blocking

These squares tend to need a pin in each corner first, then a couple more on each side close to the corner to square them nicely.

Prodigious Square

Round 24 - how to start

We're making lazy popcorns again at the corners of Round 24 but this time we're using double treble crochet to gather the stitches below.

This is where you stick your hook to make the slip stitch at the beginning of Round 24. Then you chain 4 for your starting chain or make a false double treble crochet.

Then this is how you gather the other groups of 5 stitches with a double treble crochet.

Round 25 - how to start

Again, we are making a lazy popcorn at the start, but this time we are using a double crochet and have to go back a bit to find the first 1-chain space to insert our hook into.

Super wobbly, not flat square

Don't worry! Once you do the surface crochet, your square will pull in to almost flat. A quick block will make it really straight and square. This is perfectly normal!

Blocking

This square will need pins all the way around. Start with the corners, then the middle of the sides and then pin as needed between the corners.

Round by Round Photos

Plain Square

Round 1

Round 2

Round 3

Round 4

Round 5

Round 6

Round 7

Round 8

Puff Square

Round 1

Round 2

Round 3

Round 4

Round 5

Round 6

Round 7

Round 8

Round 9

Popcorn Square

Round 1

Round 2

Round 3

Round 4

Round 5

Round 6

Round 7

Round 8

Round 9

Round 10

Prodigious Square

Round 1

Round 2

Round 3

Round 4

Round 5

Round 6

Round 7

Round 8

Round 9

Round 10

Round 11

Round 12

Round 13

Round 14

Round 15

Round 16

Round 17

Round 18

Round 19

Round 20

Round 21

Round 22 - corner

Round 22 - side

Round 23

Round 24 - corner

Round 24 - side

Round 25 - corner

Round 25 - side

Round 26 - corner

Round 26 - side

Round 27 - corner

Round 27 - side

Round 28 - corner

Round 28 - side

Round 29 - corner

Round 29 - side

About the Author

Shelley Husband is an Australian crochet designer and crochet teacher living on the south west coast of Victoria with her hubby and teenager in a tiny dot of a town by the ocean. Her two older children have left the nest and are spreading their own crafty and arty wings out in the world.

Shelley has crafted most of her life, trying "all of the crafts" over the years. These days, she spends most of her time with a crochet hook in hand. Having discovered a natural knack for crochet about seven years ago after a break of a few decades, she hasn't looked back, creating hundreds of Granny Square patterns.

Shelley loves nothing more than designing new patterns aiming to extend her own and our crochet skills, gently challenging and encouraging us to create timeless, classic pieces sure to be admired and appreciated.

Seamless crochet is a real passion and she has many tips and tricks to make our crochet look the best it possibly can, using techniques she has combined and tweaked over the years.

When not designing crochet, you can find Shelley teaching crochet in workshops around Victoria and beyond. For those who cannot make a workshop in person, she teaches worldwide via her annual Crochet-A-Long projects through her blog and YouTube channel. There is no doubting Shelley's passion for all things crochet.

You can find Shelley online on most social media channels as spincushions.

www.ingramcontent.com/pod-product-compliance
Lightning Source LLC
Chambersburg PA
CBHW061822290426
44110CB00027B/2947